Air Force Inspector General Guide to Fraud, Waste, and Abuse

FOREWORD

Fraud, Waste or Abuse (FWA) is a potential problem that can drain significant resources and ultimately rob American taxpayers. During the period of 1 October 2010 through 31 March 2011, the Department of Defense (DoD) Inspector General (IG) identified $193 million in waste, and investigations led to 140 convictions, 87 suspensions, and 99 debarments. Additionally, criminal convictions, civil and administrative settlements resulted in the return of $1.4 billion to the U.S. government.

Although these efforts within DoD are noteworthy, further improvements targeted at reducing and eliminating FWA are needed, and it isn't possible without the involvement of conscientious military and civilian personnel who identify and report questionable spending. Commanders at all levels, being responsible for both personnel and resources, must not only be able to identify signs of FWA, but must also foster an environment where FWA reduction is part of the organization's culture.

The benefits of an active FWA program are two-fold: it saves valuable resources by identifying illegal, inefficient and wasteful practices; it also makes funds available for other, better uses.

PREFACE

1. Preventing Fraud, Waste or Abuse (FWA) is public law, and DoD's efforts must be reported to Congress semi-annually. An active FWA program is not only essential for efficient and effective operations, it is also a professional responsibility and a moral imperative for every military leader.

2. The key to prevention, detection and reporting of FWA is the recognition of conditions that allow exploitation of management controls. It is important to remember that these indicators often appear as minor administrative or managerial irregularities on the surface, but the "indicators" of these conditions provide the initial warning and indicate the need for closer scrutiny by functional managers and commanders.

3. Each indicator in this guide came from audits, inspections and investigations. In a number of cases, the functional manager's recognition of the indicator was the primary reason FWA was uncovered.

4. This guide is for general information purposes only and serves to increase FWA awareness. If FWA is suspected, individuals should contact subject matter experts, their supervisory chain, commander, the IG, the AF Audit Agency or AFOSI.

5. Reporting FWA is accomplished through supervisors, commanders, the IG Complaints Resolution Process via the AF IMT FM 102, or DoD/AF/MAJCOM/ base FWA Hotline phone numbers. The AF FWA Hotline is (202) 404-5354 or (800) 538-8492 or FAX: (202) 404-5429. The DoD hotline is (800) 424-9098.

6. Recommendations for additions or changes to this guide should be forwarded to SAF/IGQ Workflow safigq.workflow@pentagon.af.mil.

INTRODUCTION

This document was designed to educate the reader about fraud, waste or abuse from an AF perspective. It starts by explaining what FWA is. Following each definition is a recommendation for addressing indications or allegations of FWA. The second chapter outlines the key roles that supervisors and commanders play within an organization while attempting to conduct efficient and effective operations.   Lastly, the guide is organized functionally, and introduces areas particularly susceptible to FWA.

Table of Contents

FRAUD, WASTE or ABUSE

FRAUD
Any intentional deception designed to unlawfully deprive the United States of something of value or to secure from the United States for an individual a benefit, privilege, allowance, or consideration to which he or she is not entitled. Such practices include, but are not limited to, the offer, payment, or acceptance of bribes or gratuities; making false statements; submitting false claims; using false weights or measures; evading or corrupting inspectors or other officials; deceit either by suppressing the truth or misrepresenting material fact; adulterating or substituting materials; falsifying records and books of accounts; arranging for secret profits, kickbacks, or commissions; and conspiring to use any of these devices. The term also includes conflict of interest cases, criminal irregularities, and the unauthorized disclosure of official information relating to procurement and disposal matters.*

RECOMMENDATION: Contact AFOSI when fraud is suspected. Failure to contact them could jeopardize an investigation. If OSI elects not to pursue an investigation due to the allegation not meeting certain monetary standards or the allegation is not deemed criminal by OSI, contact the IG, Security Forces or the AF Audit Agency to analyze the indicators.

WASTE
The extravagant, careless, or needless expenditure of government funds, or the consumption of government property that results from deficient practices, systems, controls, or decisions. The term also includes improper practices not involving prosecutable fraud.*

RECOMMENDATION: Consult the IG; conduct an internal or external inspection, Commander Directed Investigation (CDI) or Air Force Smart Operations (AFSO) 21 Continuous Process Improvement or 8-step Problem Solving event.

ABUSE
The intentional or improper use of government resources that can include the excessive or improper use of one's position, in a manner contrary to its rightful or legally intended use. Examples include misuse of rank, position, or authority or misuse of DoD resources.*

RECOMMENDATION: Conduct internal/external inspection, CDI or IG Investigation.

* Source – DoD Inspector General

This chapter discusses the unique, yet strategically important role of the commander/supervisor in preventing and detecting FWA in Air Force activities and operations. While overall responsibility for combating FWA is a function of command, most command positions are so broad as to preclude the detailed day-to-day personal involvement needed to detect fraudulent, wasteful and/or abusive actions. Regardless, the commander is ultimately responsible when these actions occur. This chapter provides 10 suggestions for fulfilling commander and supervisory responsibilities in the FWA area. Each of the subsequent sections dealing with functional-related issues should be reviewed in their entirety by all commanders as they contain items that are universal to all.

Commander's/Supervisor's Attitude Toward FWA Prevention and Detection

Commanders and supervisors greatly influence the organizational environment and actions of assigned personnel. People will generally pay closer attention to programs that the commander emphasizes. Conversely, people will ignore programs that are ignored by the commander. Therefore, the identification of FWA depends largely on commander and supervisor emphasis.

Commanders must actively promote the efficient, effective and legitimate use of AF resources under their control (AFI 90-301, *Inspector General Complaints Resolution*). To do so, commanders will:

- Establish a proactive FWA program that systematically reviews operations and processes to detect deficiencies, minimize waste, emphasize economy, and identify/correct potential fraud, waste or abuse.
- Designate within the organization, at appropriate levels, FWA Program Monitors responsible for regularly assessing the FWA climate of the organization and elevating potential FWA issues to the appropriate level of command for review and action.
- Educate all assigned personnel on what constitutes fraud, waste, and abuse with an emphasis on process improvement, adherence to AF core values, and prompt reporting of suspected violations.
- Encourage personnel to elevate/report FWA concerns to command or supervision.
- Maintain open communication channels through development of an organizational culture that discourages reprisal or retaliation against any individual making an FWA disclosure.

Importance of Standard Procedures and Controls

Over the years, the Air Force has adopted numerous procedures and controls which are designed to protect and safeguard resources. When properly followed and practiced, these procedures and controls significantly reduce an organization's susceptibility to fraudulent, wasteful, and abusive actions. Conversely, inspectors and investigators have found that most FWA occurs when organizations deviate from normal control procedures. In addition, two common reasons have been found for deviations: either people did not understand the reasons for the control or procedure, or deviations were permitted to "get the job done."

Use of Trend Reports to Monitor Operations

Evaluation of static information does not normally disclose indications of potential FWA. Rather, the evaluation of information over a period of time is more likely to disclose significant problems. Two conditions are often indicative of fraudulent or wasteful practices: (1) sudden or dramatic shifts in trends, and (2) persistent deviations from a known norm or standard.

Examples include:
A. A sudden increase in expenditures in a given organization.
B. A sudden shift in an organization's ability to fulfill their mission.
C. Persistent inventory losses in a supply operation.
D. A sudden increase in absenteeism or a perceived drop in morale.
E. Persistent out-of-stock conditions or poor service to customers/users.

Trend reports also serve as a deterrent because subordinates know the commander is interested and is getting information about an organization's operations.

Use of Independent Sources

A key control in most operations is independent reporting and evaluation. A commander can serve in the role of the independent evaluator, however it is important the information used for evaluation is not provided solely by the activity being evaluated. There are numerous sources of information available which can provide "independent" information.

Examples include:
A. Use accounting and supply staff to obtain financial/supply information about organization activities.
B. Use MAJCOM inspectors to verify adherence to regulations.

Comparative information obtained from two or more different sources is also beneficial.

Identification of Sensitive Areas

Activities and areas under a commander's purview vary significantly in their susceptibility to FWA. As a general rule, organizations which manage items that can be put to personal use or are easily sold are the most susceptible.

Manager's Internal Control Program

Air Force organizations must use cost-effective internal controls to fulfill DoD's commitment to the responsible use of resources, to comply with public law, and to ensure that resources are used properly and to their best advantage in accomplishing assigned operations and missions. Air Force Policy Directive (AFPD) 65-2, *Managers' Internal Control Program,* implements DoD Instruction 5010.40, *Managers' Internal Control Program Procedures.* The internal control program is not limited to financial resources.

Corrective Action on Inspections and Audits

A key to FWA prevention is appropriate corrective action on known deficiencies. The longer deficiencies exist, the more vulnerable the organization is to fraudulent, wasteful, and abusive practices.

Administrative and Judicial Actions

The lack of appropriate administrative and judicial actions can jeopardize a commander's ability to prevent future FWA actions. While a vast majority of people do what is right because they are conscientious, others need the reassurance that appropriate punitive or administrative actions will be taken in response to improper actions. For contractors, the mere thought of being suspended or debarred from doing business with the Government can be a deterrent in itself.

Loss, Damage or Destruction of Government Property

Air Force Manual (AFMAN) 23-220, *Reports of Survey for Air Force Property*, establishes the process the Air Force uses to implement public law and DoD guidance for the accountability of government owned property. Commanders are responsible for government real and personal property under their control. Military and civilian personnel are responsible for the proper care and safekeeping of Air Force property regardless of whether or not it is on property records. Additionally, Air Force members and employees can be held financially liable for the loss, damage, or destruction of Air Force property proximately caused by their negligence, willful misconduct, or deliberate unauthorized use.

The Commander's "Watchful Eye"

One of the most effective deterrents to FWA is the "watchful eye." Oftentimes, commanders are too busy to perform detailed analyses of operations. However, simply observing or listening serves a very useful purpose. In addition, the inquisitive commander can often spot unusual conditions needing further attention, and recognize that observations may only be symptomatic of more deep-rooted problems. The organization (wing/center) must have an active hotline program through which subordinates assist the commander in detecting FWA. Commanders and supervisors should review this guide in its entirety, regardless of functional area. Vulnerabilities such as contracting, Government Purchase Cards, travel programs, cell phone use, resource management and more that are germane to all commanders and supervisors are addressed in the following sections.

CIVIL ENGINEER

The Civil Engineers perform a wide-range of services including infrastructure maintenance and repair, and fire and emergency services, either by organic capability or by contract. Nearly all aspects of the Civil Engineer mission are susceptible to FWA. Materials, tools and equipment, which are not immediately identifiable as government property, can easily be stolen. Government construction representatives can collude with contractors. In addition, emergency services have a variety of high-value specialized equipment that could be targeted. However, if the commander promotes the right organizational atmosphere and ensures accountability, FWA can be substantially reduced.

Key Areas

Material Control
Civil Engineers are in constant contact with materials, parts, and tools that are both useful and valuable for non-military applications. These items are usually not immediately identifiable as government property and can easily be stolen. However, personnel are less likely to steal from the government if the assets are managed properly and abuses are handled appropriately. Marking equipment by etching and/or painting to identify it as Air Force property can have a deterrent effect.

Project Management
Collusion is far less likely to occur than material theft because there needs to be 2 parties involved; however, there is the potential for greater loss over a long period of time once it begins. There could be several reasons to motivate a government representative to approve substandard work or to sign for work that was never accomplished. Direct kickbacks are unlikely but possible. More likely is that a person may have a side business and receive non-monetary consideration from the contractor on non-government contracts. Another possibility, and perhaps the most common, is a lack of oversight or incompetence. One indicator there may be problems is when the government representative appears to be too friendly and/or too close to contractors. Cordiality is okay, familiarity is probably not okay.

Readiness and Emergency Management
Even though Chemical, Biological, Radiological, Nuclear (CBRN) equipment has limited value outside military applications, the equipment is expensive. Therefore, these items must be managed properly. This includes record keeping, storing items properly, and holding personnel responsible for missing/damaged equipment items.

Fire and Emergency Services (FES)
FES vehicles and equipment are expensive and must be properly inspected and maintained to ensure maximum life expectancy. The commander should apply proper oversight of FES programs to ensure compliance of published guidance.

Explosive Ordinance Disposal (EOD)

EOD personnel have access to dangerous and specialized materiel with demand in external markets. Inventory levels should be properly tracked and documented to ensure consumables are not pilfered.

Virtually all Air Force activities and organizations are supported by and rely on Information Technology Asset Management System (ITAMS) products. Unfortunately, users of these systems and products are extending them far beyond the scope of legitimate Air Force operations. Often, elaborate internal controls are developed to help reduce opportunity for misuse and, theoretically, in those instances these controls should be effective. However, even the best internal controls can be circumvented or simply ignored to satisfy an individual's motives. In the final analysis, the only real deterrents to misuse are effective management and awareness training on the part of all personnel who have access to, or use of, ITAMS equipment.

Key Areas

Unauthorized Programs Being Run on a Recurring Basis, Particularly During Hours of Low Computer Use
Programs being run that have not been authorized may be for personal benefit. Examples include programs to analyze investments or to support a business venture. Insiders, such as users, programmers, managers, and operators are prone to running such programs.

Personal Wireless Communication Systems (PWCS)
PWCS devices, including cell phones, Blackberries, pagers, and land mobile radios, are critical to timely and accurate command, control and communications. They are also expensive and easily lost or damaged. Solid management and inventory control systems will ensure these assets are accounted for and ready for use when required. Additionally, these devices can be easily used for personal business and other unauthorized uses. Strict procedures for authorization and issue, along with close monitoring of bills from service providers will help limit abuse.

Little or No Positive Control of ITAMS Assets
Often the potential to misplace or lose ITAMS assets is significant due to size and mobility. Therefore, positive control measures of ITAMS assets must be a priority and strictly enforced IAW authorized guidance or instructions. Examples include Blackberry devices and other personal wireless communication system devices.

Personnel Consistently Refuse Leave, Promotion, or Job Changes
Many times fraud and abuse are discovered when an employee is absent for an extended time (one processing cycle or during end-of-cycle processing) and substitute personnel detect an irregularity. During such absences, the perpetrator is unable to perform actions critical to avoiding detection of fraudulent/abusive practices. For example, an employee may have to input a fraudulent transaction on a recurring basis to prevent general ledger/detail record reconciliations from disclosing fund manipulations relative to accounts receivable or accounts payable.

Remote Terminals Left Unattended While On-Line

Many on-line systems such as the Data Base Management System (DBMS) have relatively simple procedures for remote users to make inquiries and also to update records. When personnel who are not authorized access to the system know how to make record inquiries and updates, a threat exists to the integrity and privacy of the data base. Therefore, remote terminal access control is crucial.

Files with Little or No Access History Being Kept On-line

Files which are seldom used can be deleted or stored on local machines. Keeping files with low utilization on disk can be wasteful, especially if it results in procurement of disk storage capacity that would be avoidable otherwise.

CONTRACTING

The United States Air Force obligates billions of dollars of taxpayer money each year through the contracting and acquisition process. The process covers how the US government purchases small commodity items through the multi-billion dollar weapon system. It is thus essential that Air Force commanders at all levels assist the Air Force to stay above board in its contracting and acquisition process.

The Federal Government follows the Federal Acquisition Regulation (FAR) as the rule book of acquisitions. The FAR clearly spells out how the government may form and enter into contracts. Generally speaking, the goal is to acquire high quality goods and services that meet the needs of the government at fair and reasonable prices. It is the responsibility of the contracting officer to use good business judgment to enter into contracts on behalf of the government.

Given the number of customers, contractors and the amount of money associated with contracting actions, FWA opportunities exist in greater numbers than other functional areas. Therefore, effective leadership and oversight is imperative to FWA prevention and identification.

Key Areas

Multiple requests for funding just below approval thresholds
In order to avoid scrutiny, personnel could split requirements and submit many smaller requests for the same or similar requirements "under the radar". Example – requestors might submit several requests over time for $24.5K to a commander whose approval authority is $25K. This action might indicate personnel are trying to split requirements or avoid scrutiny at the next level. Commanders should scrutinize all requests for requirements.

Solicitation structured so that only one contractor can win
Technical specifications or contract terms are deliberately written so that only one contractor will be able to win the future bid, even though there are other sources that could potentially fulfill the needs of the government. This action limits competition and drives up prices. There are certainly times when a unique proprietary process or a "Sole Source" situation exists, and proper justifications (signed by appropriate approval authorities) must be included in the contract file.

Companies conducting business under several different names
Company officials may attempt to conceal poor past contract performance by conducting business under several different names. Such companies may also submit more than one bid or offer in response to a solicitation, thus restricting competition. The acquisition team must know the market and contracting officers must evaluate the listing of de-barred contractors before award.

Conflict of Interest

Private business dealings or close social relationships between Air Force contractors and Air Force personnel or employees who are in positions to influence the award of Air Force contracts increases the possibility of fraud in contract awards. Close social relationships between contractors and Air Force members increase the likelihood that proposal, quotation or other contracting information might be improperly disclosed during the pre-award period to contractor personnel. It also increases the possibility that contracts are "steered" to certain vendors. This indicator applies equally to family members of Air Force personnel or employees. Air Force personnel who find themselves with a potential conflict of interest should contact the legal office or ethics counselor.

Unjustified substitutions of product or personnel

Any proposed product or personnel substitution from a contractor beyond what was originally agreed upon in a contract should be approved by the government, and appropriate compensation (from either party) should be given if necessary. For example, if a contractor bids to use a certain grade of steel in a winning bid, the government expects to receive that grade of steel in the final product.

Lax enforcement of contract provisions

Failure to enforce normal contractual requirements such as labor checks on construction contracts, starting dates, insurance requirements and contract completion dates weakens the Air Force contractual position and may allow contractors to receive full payment for less than full performance.

Multiple complaints about contractor performance

Frequent user complaints about the quality or level of performance provided by a contractor may indicate the contractor is delivering something less than the Air Force is paying for. The cause of the complaint should be investigated.

Contractor use of Government equipment or property for work outside the performance of the contract

Government furnished equipment/property should only be used for the fulfillment of a particular government contract.

FINANCIAL MANAGEMENT

DISBURSING/PAYMENTS/ENTITLEMENTS

The Finance Office performs many functions that are potential areas for FWA. All monies spent at base level finance for base operations are paid by the local disbursing office. Some of the sections each command should monitor for indicators of fraud and abuse include: public voucher payments, travel vouchers, transportation requests, civilian/military pay and entitlement transactions, and leave accounting.

Key Areas

Review of Travel Vouchers

Those who review travel vouchers, including personnel assigned to the traveler's unit, must be alert for indicators of improprieties such as:

    a. Altered lodging receipts.

    b. Hotel or credit card receipts, which include food, drink, telephone calls, etc., in addition to the lodging cost.

    c. Rooms, taxicabs, or privately owned vehicles shared with co-workers, with each claiming full rate fare, or mileage.

    d. Personnel who resided with relatives or friends and submitted false receipts reflecting lodging at hotels/motels.

    e. Traveled with spouse and submitted claims for lodging at the "double" rate rather than the "single" rate.

    f. Returned home during the TDY, but did not reflect this on the voucher and therefore collected per diem.

    g. Significant differences in claims made by personnel who traveled together.

    h. Traveler was also approving official on travel order.

    i. Lengthy leave taken over short term TDY.

    j. Excessive TDY's over weekend or holiday periods.

    k. Purpose for travel reflected on orders appears questionable or frivolous.

    l. Subordinate approves travel vouchers for superior.

Excessive Numbers of Travel Claims for Expenses that can be Accepted Without a Supporting Receipt

Personnel may be submitting fraudulent travel vouchers by including fictitious expenses that do not have to be supported with a receipt (e.g., taxi fares, dry cleaning/laundry, ATM Fees, any item under $75 threshold, etc.). Excessive numbers of such expenses in vouchers may indicate fraudulent claims.

Technicians T-Entering DTS Travel Vouchers Without Proper Documentation or Authorization to Clear Open Travel Orders on the Government Orders Outstanding (GOO) List

On a monthly basis the GOO listing is produced and reconciled to clear outstanding travel orders. To circumvent proper procedures, technicians with specific DTS access levels can clear outstanding DTS travel authorizations by processing a T-Entered travel voucher without a signed DD 1351-2, Travel Voucher as a Substantiating Record.

Ineligible Members Receiving Payments for BAH or Single Members Receiving BAH Payments at the "Married With Dependents" Rate

Employees may be in collusion with members to authorize and make payments of BAH to ineligible members or increase the BAH payment to the "married with dependents" rate for single members.

Fraudulent Receipt of BAH by Divorced Military Members

The area of concern is with the potential fraudulent receipt of BAH at the "with dependent" rate by a divorced member whose minor dependent(s) live in government quarters due to the remarriage of the member's former spouse to another service member or the member's former spouse is also a service member.

Fraudulent Government Purchase Card (GPC) Purchases.

With the GPC card becoming more prevalent as the means to buy goods and services across wings and bases the potential for FWA also increases the risk of card misuse and abuse. Collaboration between GPC Approving Officials (AO) and cardholders can lead to unauthorized purchases, therefore, it's imperative every purchase has been approved in writing by the unit commander; monthly credit card statements are reviewed and certified on a regular basis; and every purchase is accompanied with an invoice or receipt.

Report of Survey (ROS) Records Poorly Maintained and/or not Finalized.

The ROS program is an area within FM operations with a high probability for FWA. In many cases the appointed Investigating Officer (IO) fails to accomplish their responsibilities to complete an ROS which leads to unfinished reports, missing items unaccounted for, and members separating from the AF prior to collection of money when found responsible. Ensure the AF IMT 453, *Report of Survey Register*, or electronic equivalent is being maintained by the ROS manager. Make certain the IO accomplishes all assigned duties in a timely manner and submits a properly completed AF Form 20, *Repair Cost and Reparable Value Statement* with necessary supporting documents.

No Accountability of Individual Equipment Uniform (IEU) Issue for Deploying Members

Upon notification of deployment, members are given IEU letters from their unit deployment manager that allows them to be issued specified uniform and equipment items from base supply and the base service store at no cost to the member. In some instances deployments are canceled but items are not returned and funds not tracked for reimbursement. Consequently, when the member receives a second notification of deployment they are issued an entirely new set of uniforms and equipment items.

Unit Leave Records are Poorly Prepared and Maintained

Employees may be in collusion with members to alter inclusive leave dates certified by supervisors resulting in less days of leave being charged than were actually taken. Poorly prepared or maintained leave records may be kept in an effort to mask the situation.

End-of-Year (EOY) Commitments and Obligations Processing:

Miscellaneous Obligation Reimbursement Documents (MORD) are commitment documents used by units for anticipated expenses or to obligate funds for reimbursement of "potential" expenses after fiscal year (FY) closeout. MORDs can be used any time of year, but can be abused by securing funds that are not necessarily needed and could be used elsewhere. Resource Advisors (RAs) and Financial Analysts (FAs)should ensure EOY MORDs contain detailed descriptions, documentation, tracking of expected reimbursements, and unobligated funds are returned. RAs/FAs should pull an Open Document List (ODL) to review/address committed funds and outstanding MORDs.

Stock piling supplies from EOY GPC purchases is another problem area because it violates the time, purpose and amount rules set forth by regulatory guidance.

Finally, re-emphasizing the caution against unnecessary expenditures can combat the "use it or lose it" mentality prevalent at EOY closeout. Also, clearly communicating how EOY funds can be put to better use is a proactive measure to limit waste.

Employees Who are Consistently Tardy
Employees maybe falsifying their time cards if they consistently arrive for work late or depart work early and a review of their time cards indicates that they are being paid for a 40-hour work week.

Repeated Changes to Time Cards/Excessive Overtime
Repeated erasures or changes on an individual's card, amended time cards, repeated instances of prior periods of overtime earned, or little or no use of annual leave may indicate possible time card manipulation by an employee in a timekeeper position.

LOGISTICS READINESS

This chapter covers all sections that are normally found in a Logistics Readiness Squadron. While the listing is not all inclusive, it highlights some potential areas for FWA that require vigilance.

VEHICLE MANAGEMENT

A considerable amount of money is spent for the repair and maintenance of government motor vehicles and equipment. Any unauthorized purchase of parts or use of tools and shop equipment often results in an unnecessary expenditure of funds.

Indicators

Excessive Parts Replacements in Vehicle Maintenance

Mechanics/technicians may charge unnecessary parts to vehicles with open work orders and divert these parts for personal use or gain. For example, vehicle historical records that show 14 tire replacements in 8,148 miles, 5 new batteries in 100 miles or 7 tune-ups in 8,000 miles should warrant further investigation.

Government Funds Used for Replacement Parts in New Vehicles

New vehicles come with warranties that normally provide free replacement of many failed parts, meaning no cost to the government. Check vehicle historical records to see if they show any parts procured or replaced using government funds. If this type of data is found, validate parts replacement on the vehicle to ensure parts are not being diverted for personal use or gain, and government funds are not spent unnecessarily.

Unauthorized Use of Government-owned Pilferable Items (e.g. tools and equipment)

Most vehicle maintenance shops have over $500K worth of tools and shop equipment used to maintain vehicles supporting the mission. There is always the possibility personnel could use these tools and shop equipment for personal use or gain. The lack of control over these items is compounded when inventory and management control procedures are not developed. In one example, a pair of heavy duty jack stands, valued at $200, came up missing during a monthly inspection. After exhaustive search and applicable paperwork was completed, it was discovered that an individual took them home for their own personal use. In another case, members were using the government facility and equipment to perform repairs for pay on civilian vehicles.

VEHICLE OPERATIONS

Government motor vehicles (GMVs) need to be closely controlled because of their easy accessibility, high visibility, and potential for misuse. A considerable amount of money is spent for the operations and maintenance costs of GMVs and any unauthorized use results in an unnecessary expenditure of funds and potential public criticism. The Air Force cannot afford to overlook the potential for fraud, waste or abuse in its vehicle fleet.

Indicators

Frequent Complaints or Rumors Concerning Unauthorized Use of GMVs
An Operator Records and Licensing (OR&L) technician may not be recording all reported misuse cases into the vehicle misuse program.

Vehicle Returned After Usage with Excessive Miles
A vehicle operator may have used the GMV for an unauthorized purpose or to travel to an unauthorized location in order to prevent wear and tear or fuel costs of a Privately Owned Vehicle (POV).

Lost or Missing Fuel Coupons or Toll Passes
Vehicle Operations Control Center (VOCC) dispatchers may not be maintaining procedures for control and accountability of fuel coupons and toll passes. Proper controls are necessary to prevent theft and unauthorized use of government furnished fuel coupons and toll passes.

Vehicle with Excessive Fuel Card Purchases
Vehicle Operations Control Center (VOCC) dispatchers may not be maintaining procedures for control and accountability of fuel cards or personnel may be utilizing an authorized fuel card to purchase fuel for multiple unauthorized vehicles. Proper controls are necessary to prevent theft and unauthorized use of government fuel cards.

TRAFFIC MANAGEMENT
The movement of household goods (HHG) provides a lucrative area for fraud. The Air Force, with its need to move people and property worldwide, cannot afford to overlook the potential for fraud, waste or abuse in its transportation programs.

Indicators

Personally Procured Move (PPM) Movers Using a Larger Van then Necessary
Intent to defraud may be present if service members on do-it-yourself (DITY) moves request a larger trailer or van than required. The service member may want to bump the weight of the shipment to gain a profit. For example, a member could increase the weight by adding water, sand bags, cinder blocks, or other material in order to increase the amount the service member receives.

Allowing Space-Available Travel without Proof of Orders
Space-available travel procedures only requiring the service member to show an ID card, rather than also providing a set of orders, are susceptible to fraud. The member can then go PCS "free" while pocketing the travel pay.

Unusually Large Shipments of Professional Books, Papers and Equipment
Members may attempt to boost their authorized weight allowances by declaring items as professional equipment or books.

Freight Unevenly Distributed Among Carriers
Surface freight organizations are supposed to distribute freight as equitably as possible among carriers if they serve the same destination and are providing the same service within the same timeframe. Freight personnel could favor a carrier.

Freight Losses/Damages Not Documented on Bill of Lading at Time of Delivery
Surface freight personnel should annotate shortages and damages on the bill of lading at time of delivery. An employee, through neglect or collusion with a carrier, could sign a "clear" delivery thus relieving the carrier of liability.

Personal Use of Packaging and Crating Material
Many items in packing and crating are desirable for personal use (e.g., foam rubber sheets for use under sleeping bags, fastpacks for cold or hot container insulators, lumber).

Dwindling Supply of 463 L Pallets is Noted
Pallets are a costly but essential part of the 463L air-cargo handling system. Their use reduces aircraft ground time and increases airlift capability.

SUPPLY
The Air Force Supply System is a multi-million dollar business, which on a daily basis conducts high dollar value sales, receipt processing, issuance, and storage functions. If fraud amounts only to a fraction of the issuances alone, the loss could be substantial.

Indicators

Problem Areas Noted Through Report of Survey (ROS) Trends
Abnormally high trends noted on ROSs submitted for equipment accounted on Custodian Authorized/Custody Receipt List (R14) or Organizational Visibility List (R15). Equipment accounted for on R14/R15 includes sensitive and pilferable assets and could have been diverted for personal use or resale.

Local Purchases
Locally purchased supplies/equipment could be a fraud indicator if it bypasses normal ordering procedures, or the items purchased can be used for personal gain.

Items Being Transferred to Defense Reutilization and Marketing Office (DRMO)
A check should be made to ensure that items are not dropped from supply accountability before DRMO accepts item accountability. A breakdown in this procedure could result in a person stealing items under the cover of transferring the property to DRMO.

Transfer of New Items to DRMO
A person in supply could generate a transfer document to transfer an item from supply to DRMO even though a current base requirement exists for the item. This action could make new property available, at greatly reduced prices, to civilian or military conspirators acting in collusion with the supply person.

Abnormally High Consumption of Supply Items

Abnormally high consumption of common supply items with pilferage codes, such as automotive parts, tools, and individual equipment, indicates the items could have been diverted for personal use or resale.

MAINTENANCE

Nearly all aspects of Maintenance missions are susceptible to FWA, and functions cover a broad spectrum ranging from organic capability to contract services. Materials, tools and equipment, which are not immediately identifiable as government property, can be easily stolen, and Government contractor representatives can collude with QAEs. However, the right organizational atmosphere helps ensure accountability, which in turn can substantially reduce FWA.

Key Areas

"Colors of Money"
Maintenance personnel routinely use equipment funded by different streams of money. These disparate sources include flying hour, O&M and War Reserve Material Funds. The Air Force Audit agency routinely audits unit fiscal discipline. Only certain items can be purchased to support the maintenance mission using each type of funding. Ensure proper controls are in place to highlight errors and prevent abuse. Perceptions of misuse also need to be considered and properly addressed.

Material Control
Maintainers are in constant contact with materials, parts, and tools that are both useful and valuable for non-military applications. These items are usually not immediately identifiable as government property and can easily be stolen. However, personnel are less likely to steal from the government if the assets are managed properly and abuses are handled appropriately.

Project Management
Collusion is far less likely to occur than material theft because there needs to be 2 parties involved; however, there is the potential for greater loss over a long period of time once it begins. There could be several reasons to motivate a government representative to approve substandard work or to sign for work that was never accomplished. Direct kickbacks are unlikely but possible. More likely is that a person may have a side business and receive non-monetary consideration from the contractor on non-government contracts. Another possibility, and perhaps the most common, is a lack of oversight or incompetence.

Conflict of Interest
The possibility of fraud in contract awards is increased by private business dealings or close social relationships between contractors and Air Force personnel or employees who are in positions to influence the award of Air Force contracts. Close social relationships increase the likelihood that proposal, quotation or other contracting information might be improperly disclosed during the pre-award period to contractor personnel. It also increases the possibility that contracts are "steered" to certain vendors. This indicator applies equally to family members of Air Force personnel or employees. Air Force personnel who find themselves with a potential conflict of interest should contact the legal office or ethics counselor.

MEDICAL

The primary objective of the Medical Group is to maintain a healthy force to enable response to global contingency operations with short/no notice. Medics also deploy to forward operating locations during contingencies and set up mobile clinics and hospitals to provide onsite care. In addition, primary and specialty medical care is also provided to qualified dependents of military members and retirees while in garrison.

Key Areas

Overstocking perishable supplies

Sections/units in the Medical Group may be prone to overstocking perishable supplies. While the intention of the section/unit may be to prevent shortages, the carrying costs of the excess inventory as well as the waste created by throwing away expired supplies can be significant. Sections/units in a Medical Group need to accurately inventory their supplies on hand, and establish mechanisms for estimating future use rates.

Ordering unneeded equipment

Sections/units in a Medical Group ordering unneeded equipment is waste. Sections/units may order new equipment in order to have the latest high technology gadgets on hand when the existing machines still work perfectly and meet the patient care needs of the Medical Group. In addition, personnel may not be trained on how to operate the newest equipment in a timely manner, creating a situation where the new machine sits unused for a significant time period.

Not rotating expiring War Reserve Material (WRM) supplies into inventory

Perishable WRM supplies should be rotated into active inventory stocks and replenished with backfills. This rotation needs to occur while the perishable item still has enough shelf life left to have a reasonable chance at being used before the expiration date. This is particularly important with medications, which can be identical to the ones used in the pharmacy and have a high dollar value.

Equipment loss due to poor record keeping and lack of staff training

Inadequate equipment custodian training and records can lead to equipment loss. This is particularly important with mobile medical devices and information technology items. The importance of maintaining accountability for equipment assigned to a section/unit as well as conducting periodic inventories must be stressed to all medical staff members.

OFFICE OPERATIONS

Day -to-day office operations presents the most challenging environment to detect FWA as normal operations and procedures are not tracked as closely as other areas. While this listing is not inclusive, it represents some of the areas of concern.

Key Areas

Copier/Printer Management
The daily copy and printing projects are a challenge as office personnel do not typically track individual projects. The Project Manager who prints 10 copies of the same 50 page presentation or makes 100 copies of a "Luncheon" poster that could be emailed may be wasting government resources.

Supply Management
The lack of supply management at the office level is a vulnerability. Personnel taking supplies home to their children to supplement their school supplies or to run a home office may not be detected for months. Close monitoring of office supplies on a monthly basis can prevent these abuses.

Energy Management
Energy costs account for a significant portion of a base's operating cost. Leaving the lights on at all times, computers and accessories running for excessive amounts of time while not in use, or a slow water leak that goes unreported adds to these costs. Implementing office level procedures to identify these issues will eliminate waste.

Operations are susceptible to FWA in many traditional areas, such as contracting and equipment misuse, and there are some unique areas also susceptible. Materials, tools and equipment, which are not immediately identifiable as government property, can easily be stolen, and there are areas routinely perceived as waste or abuse that need properly addressed to correct misperceptions.

Key Areas

Contracted Training

QAEs should be appointed for government oversight of contracts and their activities monitored to ensure the contract is being completely and properly fulfilled. QAEs should be impartial, trustworthy advocates serving the best interest of the government. QAEs may have extensive operational background, but need supplemental training in contract oversight.

Flying Hour Program

The Air Force Audit Agency is routinely tasked to audit flying hour funds. Perceptions of misuse of flying hours also need addressed. Cross-country flights need added scrutiny throughout the leadership hierarchy to identify trends (frequent flights to the same location by the same aviator), misuse of military aircraft or conflict of interest.

Material Control

Operators (Aircrew/Battlefield Airman/Aircrew Flight Equipment) are in constant contact with equipment that is both useful and valuable for non-military applications (GPS, NVGs, All-Terrain Vehicles (ATVs), communications gear, boots, cold and wet weather clothing). These items could potentially be stolen or sold to third parties. However, personnel are less likely to steal from the government if assets are well managed and abuses handled appropriately.

Equipment Loss Due to Poor Record Keeping and Lack of Training

The importance of maintaining accountability for equipment assigned to a section/unit as well as conducting periodic inventories must be stressed to all operators assigned equipment custodian responsibilities. Equipment custodians that keep poor records or with inadequate training, can easily lead to equipment loss. This is particularly important with unique communications equipment used in operational units.

Command Buys

Purchase requests for high value equipment items, such as NVGs, body armor, or survival equipment should be scrutinized for waste potential and clear necessity. Intriguing items are also susceptible to fraud or theft due to their high demand in external markets. The importance of maintaining equipment accountability, conducting periodic inventory checks, and holding personnel accountable for damage or theft are effective tools to prevent FWA.

SECURITY FORCES

The goal of Security Forces is to protect people, property and resources of the U.S. Air Force. Their shield carries with it a certain degree of authority, and is to be worn with dignity and restraint; promoting high standards of conduct, appearance, courtesy and performance. The badge should never be utilized in such a way as to promote fraud, garner favor or condone illegal activities. The Security Forces member plays a vital role in the policing of fraud, waste or abuse at all levels within the Air Force.

Key Areas

Proper accountability and issuance of consumable XB3 items
Consumable XB3 (armament expendable) items continue to be large part of the Security Forces annual budget. In general, regardless of the category of the supply item, current Air Force policy is to use and reuse Air Force materiel to the fullest extent possible, while considering economy and safety.

Maintenance and monitoring of Intrusion Detection Systems (IDS)
While Security Forces monitor alarms and perform as Quality Assurance Evaluators (QAE) for the IDS, AFI 31-101, *Integrated Defense*, specifies that the unit or organization which owns the resource being protected is responsible for funding, installation, and maintenance. Unfortunately, many unit personnel are not familiar with IDS requirements and enter into contracts which are either not sufficient or exceed necessary security requirements.

Command Buys
High-value purchase requests for equipment items should be scrutinized. Purchases for items such as night vision goggles (NVG), body armor, and mobility equipment are intended to provide Security Forces personnel with mission-critical equipment that neutralize or mitigate anticipated threats while reducing manpower levels, staffing requirements and cost wherever possible. However, equipment should be effectively controlled and documented to ensure personnel are held accountable for damage or theft. Long term maintenance contracts should be considered to ensure high-value equipment is effectively maintained.

Vehicle Use
Security Forces personnel are entrusted with government vehicles to perform basic mission tasks. It's important that a commander understand the line between using a vehicle for work-related duties and what is considered abusive or personal use. A commander must ensure personnel understand their responsibilities, investigate suspected abuse, and punish violations appropriately.

CONCLUSION

FWA prevention is an expectation levied on us by the U.S. Congress. Prevention is possible through astute oversight and running an active FWA program. While the listings in this document are mostly wing level and not all inclusive, they are a starting point for further research while building a substantial FWA program.

Individual FWA programs should be interwoven into other efforts to promote economy, efficiency and effectiveness, such as AFSO 21 and the AF IDEA programs, as well as AF audits, and IG inspections and investigations. The overall effectiveness of each FWA program depends on the synergies created between these complementary programs, and also depends on the efforts of individuals with a vested interest in the economy, efficiency and effectiveness of operations.

Recommendations for improving the AF FWA program should be forwarded to The Inspector General of the Air Force Complaints Resolution Directorate, 1140 Air Force Pentagon, Washington D.C. 20330-1140 or e-mail safigq.workflow@pentagon.af.mil.

www.ingramcontent.com/pod-product-compliance
Lightning Source LLC
Chambersburg PA
CBHW080802290526
45790CB00008B/3557